# Stay Resourceful While You Study

TRIGGER PUBLISHING

# ABOUT THE AUTHOR

**Dr Dominique Thompson** is a multi-award-winning GP, young people's mental health expert, TEDx speaker, author and educator, with two decades of clinical experience.

She is author of *The Student Wellbeing Series* (Trigger Publishing) for young people, and co-author of *How to Grow a Grown Up* (Penguin Random House) for parents. She has done two TEDx talks: "What I Learnt from 78,000 GP Consultations with University Students" and "Understanding Why".

Dom is a Clinical Advisor for NICE and Student Minds, and a Fellow of the Royal Society of Arts (FRSA). She is President-elect of the Student Health Association, and a member of the UK government's Higher Education Mental Health Implementation Taskforce. She was lead clinical advisor for Aardman Animation's *What's Up with Everyone?* campaign.

For further information about Dom's work, visit buzzconsulting.co.uk and check outgrowingagrownup.com for parenting support and free resources.

You can also follow her on Twitter and Instagram *@drdomthompson*.

# Stay Resourceful While You Study

Make the Most of Your Student Experience

DR DOMINIQUE THOMPSON

 TRIGGER PUBLISHING

This edition published in 2024 by Trigger Publishing
An imprint of Shaw Callaghan Ltd

UK Office
The Stanley Building
7 Pancras Square
Kings Cross
London N1C 4AG

US Office
On Point Executive Center, Inc
3030 N Rocky Point Drive W
Suite 150
Tampa, FL 33607
www.triggerpublishing.com

Text Copyright © 2019, 2024 Dominique Thompson
First published as *Resourcefulness at University* and *Resourcefulness at College* by Trigger Publishing in 2019

A CIP catalogue record for this book is available upon request from the British Library
ISBN: 978-1-83796-308-9
eBook ISBN: 978-1-83796-309-6

*To everyone who supports students –
you are all heroes! Thank you!*

# ROLE DEFINITIONS

**A who's who of student support**

Doctor (general practitioner)

A medically qualified doctor who sees people in the community, not in a hospital, and is able to help with all conditions, although they may have a special interest, for example in skin problems or mental health. They are sometimes called a "family doctor", and will often refer patients to specialists, such as psychiatrists or psychologists, for specific problems.

Counselor

A counselor offers a safe, confidential space for individuals to talk. Counselors help their clients explore their thoughts, feelings and actions to help them come to terms with life and find more hopeful and useful ways to approach their future. Counselors will work in different ways, depending on their training, but will always allow their client to take the lead in what they want to talk about. They do not offer advice, but through the empathic attention they give to their client's words, the client often discovers their own wisdom, helping them to lead a more fulfilling life.

Clinical psychologist

A person who specializes in psychological or emotional conditions and mental health disorders. They will have specialized in the study of clinical psychology and will usually have a doctorate or PhD (though they're not medically qualified and will not be able to prescribe medication). They assess people and diagnose mental health conditions or problems. They are trained in using talking and behavioural interventions specifically tailored to treat psychological disorders. They may use a range of therapy approaches, including psychodynamic therapy, cognitive behavioural therapy, family and couples' therapies and interpersonal approaches. They base their assessment and treatment methods on scientific principles and outcomes and will use the best-evidenced method that helps to treat an individual.

### Therapist

A term for professionals who use talking and behavioural therapies to support people with mental health conditions.

### Psychiatrist

A medically qualified doctor who specializes in mental health conditions – also called psychiatric conditions – who can assess, make a diagnosis, offer advice and prescribe medication. A psychiatrist is the only person who can prescribe specialist medications. They work with other doctors, therapists, psychologists and counselors and will usually recommend a type of talking therapy or behavioural treatment.

# CONTENTS

**Introduction**.................................................................... 1

**Chapter 1:** Why is Being a Student So Stressful
Sometimes? ....................................................... 3

**Chapter 2:** People Problems ............................................ 13

**Chapter 3:** Health Problems ........................................... 25

**Chapter 4:** Academic Problems ...................................... 33

**Chapter 5:** Perfectionism and Time-Management
Problems........................................................... 43

**Chapter 6:** Personal Problems ........................................ 55

**Chapter 7:** "Transition Blues"......................................... 67

**Final Words** ................................................................... 73


**Additional Resources**................................................... 77

**References**....................................................................... 79

CONTENTS

# INTRODUCTION

Life is not straightforward.

There will always be challenges, difficult times and bumps in the road, so being prepared and having a skills "toolkit" for coping with these obstacles is essential.

University in particular can be a tricky time, with academic pressure, deadlines and exams, occasional relationship and friendship conflicts, or financial issues likely to impact on you at some point. The worldwide COVID-19 pandemic added to some of these challenges by disrupting social connections, creating loneliness and negatively impacting the mental health of many students, effects that linger even after life has returned to normal.

Being ready for potential problems – or at least knowing where to look for practical, relevant and reliable advice (and top tips!) if they occur – will ensure that they don't knock you off course for long. You will bounce back from any setbacks with the knowledge that you can deal with them, and you'll be even better prepared should things get tricky again.

This book is about learning those lifelong skills for bouncing back successfully.

**Who is the book for?**

This book is for any university student – or anyone preparing for university – who wants a trustworthy source of advice and information. There will be signposting to additional resources on the way and an evidence-based approach to the skills described and recommended, grounded in solid research.

This is a book that you can turn for support, to help you cope when the going gets tough and become increasingly independent and resourceful in the future.

## When will the book be useful to you?

There will of course be plenty of times when life throws you a curveball and you will manage just fine. But sometimes situations, emotions and conflicts will arise for which you feel less well-prepared and have less psychological strength to call upon at that moment.

This book is for those times when you feel like a failure or an imposter, or fear you are letting people down, or simply for when you have no idea how to have that difficult conversation with someone. Whether it's money or study worries keeping you awake at night, this book can help.

The scenarios and real-life examples might not exactly match what you are experiencing, but hopefully there will be enough similarities for you to connect with them and apply the advice to your own situation.

**This book will be useful at any time you are struggling at university – just dip in and use what's helpful to you.**

# CHAPTER 1

# WHY IS BEING A STUDENT SO STRESSFUL SOMETIMES?

It seems fair to say that young people today are under pressure like no previous generation. A whole variety of factors combine to create what can feel like a "pressure-cooker society", and it is therefore no surprise that more and more young people seem to be suffering from mental distress. Things were challenging prior to the pandemic, but the lockdowns and upset of COVID-19 have added to the issues of a generation. Being aware of some of these pressures will allow you to counter their negative effects and harness any positive angles to enhance your wellbeing.

For example, having insight into any perfectionist traits you may have will allow you to gain some perspective and reassess what might actually be "good enough" sometimes.

## 21st-century pressures

### Competitiveness

In today's world, even the fun stuff has become competitive. Often, we see things that would normally be hobbies – baking cakes, photography, writing or singing and dancing – as a form of competition. We see this everywhere and it can feel relentless.

This seems particularly true in the university or college lecture hall or seminar room, with the pressure on students to excel or graduate with honours in their degrees, rather than just gain a broad education. Sometimes, students are then pressured to do post-grad studies or get another diploma. It's a never-ending race to the top and it is exhausting for young people.

How can you try to take back some control over the uber-competitiveness of life?

- Be aware of your over-competitiveness – this is the first step!
- Choose whether or not to engage in competitiveness and when.
- Decide whether or not to participate in competitive activities beyond the obvious academic / career / sport-related ones.
- If you organize events for other students, consider not making them competitive and instead organize something "just for fun".

## Perfectionism

There seems to be a close correlation between the overly competitive nature of our society and the documented rise in perfectionism among young adults (Curran and Hill, 2017). This seems to have driven a **huge increase in the number of students with perfectionist traits** in the USA, Canada and the UK over the last 30 years.

With perfectionist traits being closely linked to several mental health conditions such as anxiety, depression, self-harm, eating disorders and obsessive-compulsive disorder, it starts to become apparent why doctors and student support professionals are seeing more students with these conditions.

In trying to keep up with everyone else, trying to be *the* best rather than simply doing *your* best, you may (in some cases) be making yourself ill.

If you're interested, and have ten minutes to spare, I even did a TEDx talk on this called "What I Learnt from 78,000 GP Consultations with University Students", which you can watch online (Thompson, 2018).

We will talk more about how to tackle perfectionism later on.

## Social media

The fact that social media can magnify issues around competitivism and perfectionism is fairly well recognized. Apps such as Facebook, Instagram or TikTok can really pile on the pressure. Not only are students driving themselves harder than ever before, but now they're being monitored and "graded" 24/7 via their own social media channels. Sometimes, people feel the need to constantly compare themselves using this medium. Social media in itself might not cause mental ill health in many cases, but it may make a difficult situation worse.

### Emma's story

Emma was a second-year student living with four other girls, all of whom were high-achieving and studying veterinary sciences, medicine or law. She felt more than able to keep up with them academically, but doubted herself constantly when it came to fashion and image. She couldn't decide what to wear, whereas they seemed to find looking good so easy and were always sharing pictures of themselves online with funny comments and hashtags. She dreaded posting anything in case she got negative comments or very few likes – or, worst of all, no reaction at all. Emma knew she was bright, yet despite being at the university of her dreams, she never felt good enough, slim enough or cool enough if she looked at her social media feeds. The pressure was making her unhappy.

For some of you, social media *will* be the source of emotional distress (e.g., seeing traumatic events online), or it might make you feel worse by fueling obsessive tendencies (driving the need for "likes" or followers) or by playing into body image insecurities.

You might want to think about how much you engage with social media if it's making you stressed, and try the following tips in order to reduce any negative impact it may have:

- Think about how much you engage with social media – are you using it too much?
- Remember that social media can be a source of support and useful resources if needed.
- Choose to follow uplifting accounts that don't make you feel inadequate.
- Limit your time looking at it by only having the apps on your laptop or computer and taking them off your phone.
- Take active steps to make time for activities and hobbies that don't require you to be online.

It's also important to:

- Uninstall apps and / or avoid websites that make you feel bad.
- Report online bullying or harassment either to the social media company itself or to your university (many now have "report and support" teams) – or both.
- Remind yourself that photos and videos are often heavily edited online to make people's lives look ideal. Try to avoid comparing yourself to what you see on your feed.
- Keep in mind that you can't always go to every social event or be part of every conversation, and that that doesn't mean that you're not still part of your friendship group (Edwards, 2019).

## Meritocracy

This is a tough one. Culturally, we are encouraged to believe from a young age that if we work really hard and give things our best shot, then we will be appropriately *rewarded* with happiness, money, success, a nice place to live, a great relationship and a happy family.

However, what this theory (that rewards are given based on merit / talent alone) fails to consider, and which can lead to us feeling like we have "failed" (because we really *did* try our best and it was *apparently* not good enough), is that *many other variables* can affect the "rewards" that we receive. Let me give you an example.

You are going to a job interview. You have the right qualifications and the perfect outfit, and you have practised answering an infinite variety of questions, perfecting your best "engaged but not trying too hard" voice and tone. The interview goes well, you don't make any giant mistakes, and you leave thinking, "Nailed it!"

But here's the thing... What you don't realize is that the lead interviewer's cat died that morning and no matter how you performed or what you did, it was never going to go well for you – or indeed, anyone else – that day.

And although the fellow interviewers tried to cheer their colleague up, it didn't work, and no one got that job.

There was nothing you could have done differently, and you still don't know what went wrong, but the point is that *despite your best efforts*, sometimes life won't work out as you expect it to.

Meritocracy can sometimes be a myth.

There are some great videos online by celebrities (Matthew McConaughey, Martin Lewis of MoneySavingExpert) illustrating this point, explaining how their success was probably talent driven, but also down to luck, who you know, being in the right place at the right time, taking risks and so on.

Just trying hard and doing your best (or even *being* the best) is not the *only* factor in success.

The message here is, therefore:

- Do your best, but accept that there will sometimes be unknown factors at play.
- Take a pragmatic and realistic approach when things go "wrong". It will allow you to bounce back far more easily next time.
- Don't tear yourself up over the job you don't get, or the proposal that fails, or the exam you score poorly in.
- Think about what went well and look at what you might do differently in future, then use that next time in the knowledge that there will *always* be an unknown element in everything we do in life.
- Remember that from some of these "failures" will come your greatest opportunities.

### Mila's story

Mila applied for a junior doctor's job in a hospital paediatric department, and of the six candidates, she was the only one not to be given one of the five posts.

She was naturally upset, but a few days later she saw a poster asking for doctors to join a 12-week expedition to Malaysia, which she would never have considered applying for if she hadn't had a period of unemployment now looming.

Mila went on the expedition, and 20 years later it remains one of the most fun, challenging, exciting and best experiences of her life. And it would never have happened if she had got that paediatric job!

## Managing your parents and carers

The lives, expectations, personal problems and beliefs of your parents and carers all impact on you as a student, and perhaps in ways you never fully appreciated until you moved to university.

Families can feel very invested in your life and future, and not just financially, of course. This can be enhanced for students from overseas, where financial investment may be very significant, or first-generation students, who may carry a weight of expectation more acutely.

Families may feel that they have a *right* to be involved in the decisions you make and the path you take, and while sometimes they may have a point (after all, they might have helped to get you to this point to a greater or lesser extent), you may not be as keen to discuss all your decisions with them – or for them to be involved at all.

### Ben's story

Ben was a 19-year-old first-year psychology student. He had been struggling with his sexual identity for a few years, had hoped that everything would be different once he was at university, and that he would be able to finally tell his family he was gay. Unfortunately, things did not turn out that way. As the year progressed, he still felt unable to speak to his father about it, despite years of distress and previous bullying at school. His mum had died when he was 11 and he did not think that his dad would accept the fact that he was gay. After a few months he decided to speak to his tutor about his worries, as the tutor seemed relaxed and open about talking with the students. With the tutor's support, Ben was able to find a website with helpful advice and came up with a plan of how to broach the topic with his dad at a calm moment.

If you can, try to find a balance between allowing family to feel a part of your life to an extent that you are comfortable with, while retaining your autonomy and independence as you establish your own identity and future plans.

Unfortunately, conflict can arise not only as students develop personal lives that challenge a parent or carer's beliefs, but also if they make academic or career choices that the family feel disappointed or confused by. For example, your parents may always have hoped you would become a lawyer, architect or pharmacist, but you want to study languages or write for a living.

Remember:

- It's *your* life and you should absolutely follow the path that will bring you fulfilment and happiness;
- But it might be thoughtful to take the time to talk to your family about your views and choices so that they feel involved and considered in the process.

This may be especially important to do if they are struggling with your decisions or you need to have a difficult conversation (see later for how to approach these).

## Talking to family and friends can be difficult

Doctors and counselors are very understanding and aware of the fact that not everyone feels able to talk to their family and friends about any worries they may have, whether academic (they fear letting people down), financial (they fear being a burden, or that they will be criticized), mental health-related (they fear being stigmatized or dismissed as "making a fuss"), or relationship-related (they worry that they won't be taken seriously or, if sexual identity is the issue, that others will be unsupportive at best, or cut them off at worst).

Talking to your closest friends and family can be challenging, but it is essential to at least consider it and try to involve them and gain their support if you can, because we all need support from other people in our lives, and they would likely be keen to help if possible.

You might even want to take them to a doctor's appointment with you, just to set the scene for them and ensure that everyone understands what is happening, if that feels relevant and helpful. Alternatively, you might spend time with a wellbeing advisor or counselor planning what to say, and when and how to say it, so that you feel as prepared as possible for a potentially tricky conversation.

**Talking to family about your worries or changes you plan to make in your life won't always make everyone happy, but at least you will have been true to yourself while being considerate of their desire to be part of the process.**

## The pandemic

The COVID-19 years had a significant impact on most young people's mental health, and for many it was a lonely and difficult time. Universities and those who work with young people are aware that you have had your normal social and academic development disrupted and may need more support to create new friendships, or study independently, in person or in groups.

You may feel more anxious about day-to-day life and meeting new people, or you may struggle with the workload at university, having not had the "normal" preparation for studying at a higher level. The good news is that you will not be alone in wrestling with these challenges, and a lot of new help and support has been developed by institutions to connect students, create new social groups, teach people how to study on their own and build confidence.

It won't always be easy, but if you can take advantage of the opportunities offered to meet your course mates or learn in person, then you will flourish and be much less likely to feel lonely or academically isolated.

**In summary**

All of these different 21st-century pressures and demands can really build up at a time of transition and academic expectation, so be kind to yourself. Take the time to think about the challenges and consider how to respond or react for the best outcome.

In the next few chapters, we will consider the most common problems that students encounter, what some real-life examples might look like, and which possible solutions or strategies you might use to deal with them.

# CHAPTER 2

# PEOPLE PROBLEMS

Relationship ups and downs are a part of life, and learning to recognize when things are going wrong and how to address them is a skill that takes time to develop. It isn't always easy to get right. Some people will always find it difficult to address this sort of interpersonal discord in their lives, but hopefully some of the tips below will help you to think about those situations that are stressing you and give you some ideas of what to do about them.

## Conflict in friendships / relationships / with housemates or roommates

There is no doubt that a significant amount of the distress caused to students at university is from conflict in relationships with others, whether it be from making new friends, leaving old friends behind (or finding that people you'd hoped to have left behind have turned up at university with you!), or learning to live with strangers from around the world. Perhaps issues arise in communicating with romantic partners (or those you *hope* will be intimate partners!), or the recurring nightmare of group relationships, which can be destabilized by individuals or cliques (this can be in relation to living arrangements, group work on your course, or friendship groups).

This might include dealing with:

- Slovenly housemates
- Cheating partners
- Unkind or unthoughtful friends
- Overbearing parents
- Irritable or demanding academic staff

More worryingly, it might also include aggressive partners, risky behaviour by others that impacts on you, and even violence or assault in some (rare) cases. If these scenarios are happening in your life or your friends' lives, you will need professional support and advice, so don't hesitate to ask for help. Plenty will be available.

Specifically on the subject of sexual assault or harassment, many universities now have trained advisors who deal only with such cases and can be contacted through university websites or reporting tools such as "Report and Support". It is really important to seek help if this has affected you in any way – **you are not alone.**

### Housemates' example

Ted, Andy, Beth and Saira were living together in their third year and got along pretty well. Then Beth met Richard, and the two of them started spending a lot of time together. Richard seemed to be at the house more and more often. He shared their food, used their bathroom, slept over, and soon it seemed like there were five housemates, but only four of them were paying the bills and buying the food. Nobody wanted to say anything initially, but eventually Saira mentioned it to the boys, and they agreed that it was irritating all of them. They liked Richard, and were happy for Beth, but this was stretching their patience. They decided to have a "difficult conversation".

For many scenarios, utilizing the following skills might be a good place to start.

## How to have "difficult conversations" – basic conflict-resolution skills

These skills might prove useful throughout your life!

*Avoiding* conflict or difficult situations may sometimes seem like the easier option, and we all do it, but it might be that the best path to take is the one that is tricky *now*, and it will hopefully lead you to a better long-term end result.

Remember that (in general):

- People want to be understood, listened to, and heard. Start with this in mind when you are having a difficult conversation.
- People might feel threatened or become over-emotional.
- There may be stuff going on for them that you are not aware of, whether or not they choose to share that with you.
- There are always two sides to every story; even if you strongly believe your side to be the most morally or ethically right, there may be additional factors that you are not yet aware of.
- We all occasionally have to get **comfortable with being uncomfortable** – in this case, living with a less-than-ideal situation. Remember, everything is a phase (more on this later). It's temporary and will be over soon. In the meantime, focus on what matters most to you and keep going!

**Top tips on having a difficult conversation**

- Pick a good time, not when people are just going out / coming in, exhausted or caught unawares. Mention that you'd like to talk and agree a time that suits you both.
- Be compassionate, whenever possible.
- Listen *actively*; hear what they are *really* saying. Read their body language too.
- Try to avoid aggressive language / swearing and so on, as it really raises the stress levels and rarely achieves anything helpful.
- Communicate clearly what you are trying to say and perhaps plan the **three key points** you want to make in advance.
- Be prepared to compromise or agree on something slightly less than ideal in order to resolve the situation. It might not be perfect, but you should feel able to live with the decisions made.
- Sometimes it is impossible to sort a problem out or agree on a solution, in which case you might need to let that one go and **agree to disagree** in order to move on with your lives.

### If the feelings from conflict or difficult relationships are overwhelming

Some people are particularly sensitive to conflict with others and take perceived slights and criticism badly – perhaps even out of proportion – or they can misread communications from friends or partners, leading them to feel extremely distressed or even to harm themselves.

If you recognize this reaction in yourself it may be helpful to talk to a healthcare professional like a doctor, psychologist or counselor about it, as you might find that learning specific skills through therapy may be useful for future relationships.

In the immediate aftermath of self-harm there is support available from organizations such as Samaritans, or Crisis Text Line (USA and international options) or other websites or apps designed to help you (see the resources at the end of the book).

This is not just a "young person thing" either; I have spoken to several academics and university staff over the years who have suffered with these feelings and self-harmed. An important aspect of recovery has been their ability to seek help and professional therapy, though sometimes it has taken them years to do so. They all say they wish they had got help sooner.

## Difficulty making friends or meeting new people

It's not uncommon for students to book a doctor's appointment because they "don't have any friends". It's always quite saddening, and doctors often wish that they could prescribe social activities to help them meet likeminded people to make new connections.

In some ways, of course, universities *do* provide a variety of opportunities to meet new people, but it can be particularly challenging to do this if you are autistic or have social anxiety, for example.

Many people from all sorts of backgrounds and cultures can struggle to connect with others, but the wonderful thing about arriving at a new place is that there are literally thousands of people all looking to make new friends, learn new things and try new experiences. You will find "your people", but it can take time.

Why does having friends matter?

Social connectedness is recognized as a really great way to stay healthy and mentally strong (Jose, Ryan and Prior, 2012), so even if you quite like your own company, it may be good for you to connect with other people occasionally. Feeling a sense of belonging, of being linked to others and having a role, helps us to stay well and find our purpose in life.

**In other words, people who are well-connected to others socially have been shown to have greater wellbeing in life.**

Whether at home, at school, at work or in the community, it is well worth finding other people you enjoy spending time with.

So, let's have a think about how you might make some new connections.

---

### Top tips on making connections

Not everyone finds it easy to connect with others, so here are some tips that might help.

- **Get out there!** Say yes to invitations to meet up, to charity fundraising, to sporting events, to gigs. Try them and see if there's anyone there who sees life like you do. It doesn't have to be a proper invitation either; just seeing an advert for an event is fine. Show up and see what happens – the key is to get out of your room! Since the pandemic, a lot of students tend to stay in their room more, not even going to lectures, which means that they are missing out on lots of opportunities to meet people. Whenever you can, try to get out and about.
- **Use social media** to find out about events etc., but don't use it instead of actually seeing people face to face. Having friends online is fine but should not replace the very real human need to have friends in person too. Once you have connected with people online you may want to meet up with them later on.

- **Smile!** It's a wonderful way to break the ice and make you seem like a nice person who others would like to speak to and be friends with. Similarly, say hello in corridors, even to strangers. It doesn't have to be weird; just a quick "Hi!" and a brief smile is a start, and people will subconsciously file you in the "Good People" category of their brain.
- If you are autistic, neurodivergent or have other specific challenges, then **check in with your university support teams**, who often organize get-togethers that are sensitive to particular needs. Many universities cater specifically for neurodivergent students with alternative Welcome Week activities or clubs. They will also know which other local organizations hold events or gatherings in the area, like a quiet pub meet-up, or quiz night and pizza, if that's what you prefer. It doesn't have to include alcohol either!
- **Join societies** that provide the activities you enjoy (or even try a completely new one) – whether it's politics, rugby, crochet or baking, there seems to be something for everyone!
- **Join the student radio or newspaper teams**; you can just help out, make tea, suggest ideas and be in the background initially, if you're shy.
- **Volunteer!** This is an amazing way to meet new people, who are very likely to be friendly, kind and compassionate. And you will be helping others too, which is always a bonus! Check out local volunteering opportunities online or via your Students' Union.
- **Read articles** like "The Science of Making Friends as an Adult" by Vanessa Van Edwards, which explains how we can connect with others without coming over as too needy or weird.

## Arjun's story

Arjun had always been shy. He'd had a close group of friends at school, but found he was struggling to meet people at university. Everyone seemed so confident and bubbly. It was a bit unnerving. The first few weeks passed, and although he was going to lectures and people were friendly enough, he hadn't really made any good friends yet. He called home after a month and mentioned it to his mum. She was naturally concerned for him, but suggested that he volunteer through the Students' Union, initially to get out and about and see his new city a bit more, but also to meet some like-minded people. She also suggested joining the chess club and martial arts' societies, since he had enjoyed these activities at school.

He had been reluctant to go along on his own, but with his mum's encouragement and a "What's the worst that could happen?" ringing in his ears, he followed both of her suggestions in the next week. He even discovered a martial art that he'd never heard of before, and over the next few weeks and months he gradually made a core group of three or four good new friends with whom he could spend time.

## Responding to peer pressure

When you arrive at a new university, it is usual to want to try to fit in, settle down and feel like part of the crowd. Many students then find that they feel pressured to participate in activities such as drinking alcohol, taking drugs (including study drugs) or having sex when they don't feel comfortable or ready to do so. They worry that if they don't join in, if they say no or are seen to be the odd one out, that they will be ostracized, isolated, mocked, or cut out of the friendship group.

Obviously, none of those options are appealing when you have just arrived somewhere new!

The reality is that fewer young people are drinking and using drugs. It may be helpful to know that recent figures show that an increasing number of students – up to a third in the UK in 2022 (Cushnahan, 2022) and over a quarter in the US (University of Michigan, 2020) – are "teetotal" (choosing not to drink alcohol at all), and fewer young people than before are using drugs in the UK (6 in 10 students, according to a survey by the UK Higher Education Policy Institute (Higher Education Policy Institute) in 2018, had *never* used drugs). In the US, the number of university students using drugs has risen in recent years, but 55% do not use drugs (Bouchrika, 2023), so you will still be in a majority if you decline.

In other words, if you choose to be moderate or careful in your approach, you will **not** be alone. So how can you say no in a way in which doesn't make you feel uncomfortable? There are a number of options you can try.

---

**Top tips on dealing with peer pressure**

- Respond with a clear, "No thank you".
- If you feel you can't do this, give another reason or even a small white lie (such as "I'm on antibiotics" or "I get migraines").
- Make a joke to diffuse the pressure.
- Get a friend to back you up if there's any resistance.
- Suggest an alternative activity.
- If all else fails, you can make your excuses and leave ("I'm feeling ill / tired / sick" / "I've got an early lecture" and so on).

**Remember**, genuine friends will never push or force you to do things you don't want to do, so if there is continued pressure, it may be time to find new friends.

## Dealing with moral dilemmas or difficult decisions about life

Uni life is a time of change and looking to the future and can be filled with all sorts of difficult decisions – where to live, where to look for work after university, whether to study after your course finishes and so on.

Moral dilemmas may also arise where you just don't know what to do. Your course-mate's partner makes a move on you, for example – do you tell your friend?

---

### Top tips on making difficult decisions

- Write a list of pros and cons to each.
- Talk issues through with others who you trust.
- Another handy technique is **to have a conversation with yourself.**

The latter technique is where you talk things through in your head, rationalizing or arguing them out with yourself. You could perhaps even unleash your inner four-year-old and ask yourself "Why?" a lot, in order to reflect on how a situation is making you feel in general.

This can be great if you're wrestling with a moral dilemma or a problem in your life, such as whether or not to tell your roommate that you saw her partner kissing someone else last night (this seems to happen a lot!).

Try this:

**Me:** Hmm, I don't think I should see John anymore.

**Also me:** But if I dump him, I'll be alone forever and have no one to hang out with when everyone else is all paired up! Why would I do that?

---

| | |
|---|---|
| **Me:** | But he's making me stressed and unhappy when he doesn't do what he says he'll do, like be on time, call me, message me, and come out with my friends when he said he would. |
| **Also Me:** | But those are small things; it's not like he's aggressive or mean, so why am I being so picky?! |
| **Me:** | But it shows he doesn't respect me! He doesn't value my time and he's being careless with my feelings. |
| **Also Me:** | But I'll be alone! |
| **Me:** | Better to be alone for a while than with someone who doesn't really care about me. Okay. Maybe I'll talk to him about how I'm feeling, and see if he is keen to make more of an effort and do as he promises; that's a good place to start... |

This can also be a useful technique if you are alone, either at home or abroad, with no one immediately available to take the other side of the conversation. So, for example, "Shall I take that intern role? They're not offering a salary, but the experience would be amazing... but I need the money too." And so on.

The conversation techniques in the box above are actually recommended by psychologists to help us think things through and avoid making rash decisions. We need to ask ourselves awkward questions like "Why am I finding this difficult?" in order to process feelings, and even to consolidate learning.

So, the next time you are having a dilemma or feel like you're in a tight spot, try having a conversation with yourself and calmly think through what's going on for you at that moment.

# CHAPTER 3

# HEALTH PROBLEMS

## Mental health

The current generation of students is much better educated about mental health and wellbeing and is much less likely to stigmatize either themselves or others than previous generations.

Having said that, there can still be real barriers preventing people from getting the help they need. These could be concerns about what others will think, the potential effect on vocational courses and "Fitness to Practise", or simply not realizing that there is a health problem in the first place. This can lead to significant difficulty accessing the care required when people *do* seek help (because of waiting lists and so on).

The current wave of students seems to be experiencing more mental distress than previous generations, even before the pandemic, and much has been said about why that might be, so if you are worried about your own mental health or that of a close friend, then don't hesitate to discuss your concerns with a professional.

**Top tips for seeking help**

- Your university will have multiple services set up to support students, so if you're not sure where to start, check the university website or ask your academic department staff / tutor for guidance about where to go.
- Look up "Student Support Services". Your residential / accommodation teams will also know where to signpost you to.
- The key is not to hide away and suffer in silence, but to talk to someone in a position to help you, such as a doctor, wellbeing advisor, psychologist or counselor, and start the conversation. Whether it's about your own wellbeing or that of a friend, they will have dealt with such issues hundreds of times before. The reason they work in a university in the first place is usually because they want to support students, so please do approach them.

## A word about carer students (students who care for other students)

Many students also support other students, and some become carers for their partners, or housemates. This can place a huge pressure on the carer student at a time when they have many other pressures to balance, as well as potentially leading them to develop a mental health condition.

The support provided can vary from looking after a housemate's antidepressant medication to ensure that they don't take too much, to constantly accompanying them to classes, appointments and activities. It can be exhausting, but students can be incredibly generous and self-sacrificing without realizing the potential negative impact it may then have on their own wellbeing.

If this is you, then there may be support available at your university for carers, so do ask either the doctor, counseling service, or other student support teams what's available to help you – and, of course, to find additional support for the student you are caring for.

## Food and healthy eating

It can be surprisingly tricky to eat well and healthily at university. Whether the catered food is not to your taste, or self-catering means that you let the food shopping slide to focus on your essay, or that you exist on takeaways for weeks at a time through exam season, getting your vitamins, fibre and "brain food" can prove complicated. Anxiety and stress can also have bad effects on your guts.

Lots of students go to see the doctor with constipation, irritable bowel syndrome (IBS) or related bowel symptoms, and often all that is needed is a bit of time spent thinking about some better food choices: the right kind of fibre, eating something that "doesn't have a label on it" (i.e. it's fresh and not out of a packet or store-bought / ready-made), and drinking enough water (staying well hydrated).

---

### Top tips for healthy eating

Don't wing it, plan it!

There are various ways to achieve a healthy student diet, such as:

- Planning shopping deliveries
- Buying and using simple cookbooks
- Joining culinary Students' Union societies
- Keeping fruit in your room (and actually eating it, not just using it as an ornament!)
- Sharing a cooking rotation with roommates
- Cooking in bulk at weekends then freezing it for the week ahead
- Planning your budget

---

But the key is to *actively* think about it. Spend some time planning ahead and setting things in place, then get on with other things, knowing that the food / recipe shopping / cooking rotation / extra vitamins are taken care of. It can be really helpful to share this aspect of student life with other students, for example sharing a regular food delivery or recipe ideas.

If you are having possible stress-related bowel symptoms (irregular bowel habit, bloating, wind and tummy pains), a simple strategy may be to try a FODMAP diet initially (designed for irritable bowel syndrome-specific relief, see the resources at the end of the book) and see if that helps. If things aren't any better after four weeks, then please see a doctor. If you are worried about your symptoms, then definitely don't ignore them. Get yourself checked out by a nurse or doctor!

It is worth remembering that eating issues or eating disorders can start – or get worse – at university, often because eating patterns can become chaotic or because stress levels rise. So, if you are worried about your eating, or even not sure what's going on with your food and eating behaviours, then seek advice and support early. Don't wait for things to deteriorate.

### Advice on sleep

We all underestimate the importance of sleep, and yet the best-selling book *Why We Sleep* by Matthew Walker has, in the words of one reviewer, shown "how a good night's shut- eye" can make us "cleverer, more attractive, slimmer, happier, healthier and ward off cancer... it's probably a little too soon to tell you that it saved my life, but it's been an eye opener" (O'Connell, 2017).

Missing out on sleep, the book says, can have a catastrophic effect on our health and wellbeing.

Doctors often tell students that rather than resorting to study drugs, as many do in order to stay awake and work longer, they would be better off getting a good night's sleep and then having a cup of coffee in the morning if they need it.

If you want to learn more about how sleep makes us better at learning and remembering things, you might also like to watch Russell Foster's brilliant TEDx talk, "Why Do We Sleep?".

So, how do we get a good night's sleep?

Well, first of all, before we get into the "sleep rules" it's important to understand that sleep is a *habit*, and so if it has been "broken" and you are not sleeping well, or if you have been sleeping in the day and staying up all night, then it will take time to reset your biological clock and get into a good habit.

About six weeks of following the upcoming sleep rules should do it, but if you're still struggling after that, talk to a doctor or therapist about it. Don't suffer in silence.

Insomnia and disrupted sleep patterns can be absolute torture. Rest assured, most doctors still remember the horror of junior doctor life, going for days without sleep, or working nights for long stretches, so they'll have every sympathy! Please do not ignore this essential wellbeing function, especially as it helps improve the quality of your academic work, as well as keeping you healthy.

---

### Top tips – the "sleep rules"

- Try to go to bed and get up at the same time every day, Monday to Sunday. Use your alarm, if necessary, to set the routine!
- Try to be asleep when it's dark and awake when it's light – but within reason; midnight to 8am, for example. Don't sleep in the daytime or stay up all

night to work; you need **about eight to nine hours' sleep a night** as a young adult.

- If you have to nap in the day, then do it before 3pm and make it short – less than an hour long.
- Stop all work and turn off all screens at least one hour before bedtime.
- Spend that hour winding down, chatting with a friend, listening to quiet music, having a warm bath, reading quietly, or watching TV (nothing too scary or exciting!).
- Exercise in the daytime before about 6pm, and don't have caffeine or alcohol late in the evening; nor should you eat any heavy meals late (although light snacks are ok).
- Create a gadget-free zone. That means no lights that might blink at night, no notifications lighting up the room, and no clocks that you can stare at when you should be sleeping.
- Don't lie in bed awake for hours. If you can't get to sleep, get up, do a relaxing activity for a while, and, when you feel sleepier, try to get back to sleep (MedlinePlus).

Stick to these rules for about four to six weeks, and if that isn't working then check out Cognitive Behavioural Therapy for Insomnia (CBT-I), which is proven to improve sleep, as well as making time to talk to a professional about how you are doing, as there may be other things you can try that can help to improve your sleep and mood. They can also help address any underlying issues that may be leading you to lie awake at night.

## Returning to studies after an absence

Many students (at all levels of study) have to take time out for ill health (mental or physical), family issues, bereavements, pregnancy, and sometimes because they have lost all motivation and need a leave of absence in order to regroup and regain their perspective on life. It is probably fair to say that not enough students take a leave of absence when they need to, and that more might benefit from making the most of the university systems in place to help them take a break when it becomes necessary.

Most of these students return to higher education after their break feeling refreshed and recovered, and with renewed enthusiasm for their studies, but it can occasionally be tricky to settle back into student life. This might be because they have experienced a different pace of life in which they have had more or less freedom, or they have a new health condition to manage, or their friends have all moved on to the year above or have graduated, or simply because of changes in the university environment.

> **Top tips on returning to university**
>
> Adjustment to any change takes time and can be difficult, so it may help to prepare for a return to your studies by:
>
> - Communicating in advance with friends you might socialize or live with upon your return.
> - Contacting your academic tutors to ensure that you have any reading lists or to get ideas about what to study in advance.
> - Considering a "back-to-school" day or weekend visit in order to physically experience the campus / housing options and check out any alterations or unforeseen changes on campus that might otherwise trip you up emotionally.
> - If you are going to need medical care or psychological therapy, then it can be helpful to liaise with the

medical team or counseling service in advance of your
return and set the appointments up ready for your
arrival.
- All universities have Access or Disability units, so you
  might like to contact them and see what they might be
  able to offer you in order to ease your transition back
  into university life. You won't know until you ask!

With some preparation and planning, a return to studying
should be smooth and relatively uneventful, but it can help
to adjust expectations prior to returning, as life may be a
little different (in both good and less good ways) on settling
back in.

# CHAPTER 4

# ACADEMIC PROBLEMS

## Academic pressure

Academic work is undoubtedly one of the greatest burdens felt by students.

The regular assessments; the competition with highly competent peers in the subject (i.e., perhaps you are no longer the top of the class); the overt competition and discussion of exam questions, results and grades by other students; the feeling that you are investing so much energy, time and possibly money in your degree or studies so you can't risk failing; the expectations of parents... All of these are genuine pressures than can potentially create enormous strain throughout your time at university.

---

### Top tips for managing stress

There are several ways to manage academic stress and ensure that you don't let it overwhelm you:

- Check out academic skills workshops and learn about the most effective ways to study and learn.
- Ensure that you have a good work-life balance and care for yourself properly throughout your time at university. This may include checking out some

---

- self-care tips such as blocking time off to relax, seeing friends or exercising.
- Ask for academic support from university staff, who are there to help you and ensure you reach your academic potential (it's literally their job!). Additional support has been created for students by many academic departments after the COVID-19 pandemic.
- If you are struggling, then **don't ignore it**. Talk to the student support services and address the problem before it becomes a crisis.

## Academic pressure can be high risk

There are many things that stress students out, but academic pressure is one of the greatest concerns. It has been shown to be linked to a heightened risk of suicide in young people under 20 (National Confidential Inquiry into Suicide and Safety in Mental Health, 2017), and in students specifically it has been shown that suicide may be associated with exam times at university (peaking in September and April) (National Confidential Inquiry into Suicide and Safety in Mental Health, 2018).

So, if you're feeling the strain, please don't keep pushing on, crushed under the weight of your degree. Talk to someone and let them help you to lighten that load. You're not alone, and help is available. You are not letting anyone down and it is not "failure" – we all need help sometimes.

### Roshni's story

Roshni was a 23-year-old international student, studying for a master's. Her tutor had noted that she looked dishevelled and was very quiet in seminars, so they encouraged her to have a chat.

Roshni said that she had been feeling low for months, but her parents "didn't believe in mental health" so she had not felt able to speak to them. She did not feel comfortable talking to her housemates about herself, and didn't have many friends at the university.

Academically, she was worried about a presentation which was coming up. She asked her tutor for help, and they were happy to listen.

The tutor was very supportive and compassionate. They sat with her as she made a doctor's appointment to discuss her low mood, reassured her about the presentation, and talked about how she could gain confidence in her academic work by going to some skills groups being run in the department. They told her that she was not alone and that they would meet with her each week. She felt happier and reassured by these first steps to getting back on track.

## Procrastination

Have you tidied your room for the fifth time, put all your books in alphabetical order, then colour-coordinated your sock drawer? Have you doodled, made lists and updated all your social media accounts? Have you slept till you can't sleep anymore? Do you recognize yourself in the wheel of suffering (on the next page)?

Then you are definitely procrastinating!

We all do it. Staring at a blank screen or page, not knowing where to start with an essay, having "writer's block", feeling like you have to read *everything* about a topic before you can start writing about it or designing your project... There are so many ways to feel defeated before you've even started your work. Some neurodivergent students with Attention Deficit

Hyperactivity Disorder (ADHD) can find time management and planning tasks particularly difficult, so procrastination can be a bigger issue for them.

Procrastination is a common problem at university, whether you're a student or an academic. On the plus side, because it is such a well-recognized issue, entire workshops and skills classes are run in most universities to help you get back on track, so definitely check out what is available where you are and sign up for one.

Do you recognize yourself in the Procrastination Wheel of Suffering?

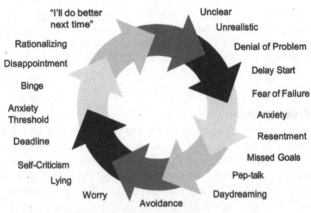

*With kind permission to reproduce by Dr David Rasch.*

**Top tips for overcoming procrastination**

Here are a few tips to get you started while you book yourself into a procrastination / academic skills / writing masterclass (with thanks to Abby Shovlin, and Rasch, 2018):

1. Start writing **something** – anything. Start in the middle, write a paragraph, go back to the beginning, write the ending – it doesn't matter; just write **something**. Even if that all gets lost / deleted in the final draft, you have to start somewhere.
2. Remember that nobody ever writes the final draft straight off. Your essay / project / idea / thesis will **evolve**. The final draft may look nothing like your first draft!
3. It takes time, but start with something on the page in front of you. It doesn't need to be perfect, or even relevant to the final product. Seeing something written in front of you will then allow you to think about it **outside of your head** and critique it or expand upon it. This **"brain dump"** can then lead to analysis and planning.
4. Write an **"elevator pitch"** of your idea – that is to say, see if you can summarize what you're trying to do in one or two sentences. Then expand on it. (Use mind maps if they help here.)
5. Learn about **active reading**. This skill can be very useful for analysing what you read, asking questions of the text as you go along, then thinking about how what you have just read could be interpreted or useful for what you want to produce, write or create (Open University, 2018).

## A word about "going blank in exams"

This is quite common and happens when you suddenly feel really anxious about the exam. There are a few things you can do to **reduce the likelihood of the mind blank** happening in the first place, and also to manage it if it does happen.

1. **Get a good night's sleep**. Sleeping well before exams is sometimes tricky, but a good night's sleep *after* a day of revising actually helps to consolidate all your learning and seal those facts into your memory, so making sure that you get your eight or nine hours of shut-eye is key throughout your revision.
2. **Revise in a variety of locations** so that when you are then in the *exam* location, you are less put off by the new environment. So, revise in different libraries, coffee shops, at home and so on, keeping your brain on its toes by changing your surroundings regularly (Carey, 2015).
3. Equally, revise in situations that are **not** all peaceful and relaxing in order to prepare yourself for the anxiety and stress scenario of the exam. Get used to working where there are occasional noises or activity around you, so that you train your brain into focusing **despite these distractions**. It doesn't need to be a combat zone, just not always a library!
4. Learn some **relaxation techniques** such as mindfulness, or just good old-fashioned breathing exercises in order to bring your anxiety under control and overcome the mind blank.

## Top tips for general exam preparation

- Don't leave it all until the last minute: plan your revision and stick to that plan.
- Use flow charts, diagrams and images – we learn brilliantly when we use visual aids!
- Practise old exam papers and questions.
- Explain topics to people who don't study them with you (or to your family), as having to explain something helps us to understand it better.
- Take breaks for at least ten minutes at a time. Stretch, walk around, or get outside and get some vitamin D from the sun on your skin.
- Eat sensible, healthy food and stay hydrated. And don't skip breakfast on the day of the exam!
- Plan for the day of the exam: note down where it is, timings etc. (Yes, doctors have been asked for a note by someone who missed their exam because they "got lost on the way", and no, they don't write one!)
- Don't just copy out your lecture notes; read them, then write down what you remember for better long-term recall.
- If you like studying with others, work in a group and explain things to each other.

## Lack of motivation / energy for work

Getting started on something can be hard enough when you have some ideas and enjoy your subject, but when students feel unmotivated and exhausted, lacking in energy or enthusiasm, then it can be near-impossible to get anything done.

It is not uncommon for students to seek help and advice from healthcare and support professionals for lack of motivation and apathy.

It can, of course, be part of a bigger problem such as **depression**. So, if you have also lost interest in doing the things you used to enjoy, and feel flat or down, or have poor sleep etc. for more than a week or two, then you must seek advice, preferably from a doctor initially.

And we mustn't forget that some medical conditions such as an **underactive thyroid** can also cause issues with energy levels and motivation, so that might need a check-up too.

---

**Top tips to combat a lack of motivation**

If other possible causes have been ruled out, and your lack of motivation is more about your studies and course itself (you hate it, the topic is dull, you didn't want to study it in the first place, it was a second-choice option, your parents wanted you to do that subject etc.), then it may be helpful to **speak to someone in the university's careers department, or to an academic advisor**, for whom these issues make up a significant part of their daily workload.

There may be options you had not considered before or realized were even possible, such as:

- Trying a new or different module
- Changing courses
- Exploring opportunities to travel abroad
- In some cases, considering a change of university if necessary

You just need to ask for guidance and talk to the professionals about the problem you are having. After all, helping students to successfully complete a degree they enjoy and achieve their potential is literally their day job!

---

Try this:

Take a moment to **remember why you are doing what you are doing, and try to visualize what life might be like when it's done**.

Visualization is a technique that some people find useful for focusing on a positive future scenario, instead of focusing on things that are not going well or are frustrating. Having a mental image of where you want to be or what you want to achieve can be a powerful way to help you get there, but you have to act on it too. If you are feeling stressed and need to remind yourself why you are doing what you are doing with all the effort it entails, visualization allows you a moment to breathe and refocus.

---

**Top tips – visualization**

- Make sure you are in the right frame of mind, calm and ready to focus.
- Take time to build an image or vision of what life might look like, where you might be, what you might be doing, if things went well and worked out. It might be you walking up to collect your degree, it might be you in a great job, or travelling somewhere exciting because of your degree...
- Ask yourself: what would have to be different and what might need to change to get you there?
- Try to feel excited or positive emotions about what you are imagining.
- Don't rush, enjoy the images and let yourself believe you can achieve these things.
- Keep visualizing at different times – practise visualizing to keep yourself on track and motivated.

**Remember!**

Universities exist (mainly) to educate people and award degrees – they want (and need!) you to be successful and happy with your course. So, engage with the staff to make sure you are!

# CHAPTER 5

# PERFECTIONISM AND TIME-MANAGEMENT PROBLEMS

## Perfectionism

Voltaire is often slightly misquoted as having written "Perfect is the enemy of good".

But take a moment to think about what he was saying. What he meant was that when we strive for perfection, we lose sight of (or ignore) what is "good" and "good enough". We can exhaust ourselves trying to be the best and make everything perfect when we could have achieved enjoyment and satisfaction with our activity / work by making it good enough.

In a world where perfectionism is on the increase, it can be hard to maintain a perspective on what is **good enough**. But being able to accept "good enough" might actually be what saves your sanity and keeps you healthy.

If you work hard on something, give it your best effort and are pleased with what you have achieved, then try not to be derailed by others talking about their work, or their exam answers, or their projects, which can then lead you to feeling as though you should have done something differently.

Don't let others shake your confidence, and don't let their competitiveness drive you toward perfectionism. Learn when to stop working, and be pragmatic and say, "That's enough, I've given it my best shot, and I'm okay with that."

What does perfectionism look like?

- Are you the person who gets 95% in a test and spends hours wondering what happened to the other 5%?
- Do you berate yourself for not getting top marks in a test, when in fact it was all new content and really tough for everyone?
- Are you highly self-critical if you don't come top, or if you don't consider your work to be perfect? Are you quite often late to hand work in because you are redoing it or still trying to make it perfect?
- Do you see your work only in extremes, either "perfect" or "the worst"?
- Do you aim for perfection from the beginning of a piece of work, and so delay, procrastinate and faff about because it's not perfect immediately?

This is what perfectionist traits look like. They can be highly destructive for your wellbeing, as you can sometimes undermine yourself with your negative self-perception.

Perfectionism can lead to students either **avoiding** the work or activity completely, or **overcompensating** (such as feeling that you need to check your work six times, otherwise you will make a mistake, and everyone will judge you).

## Zack's story

Zack was a very creative humanities student. He only had a few weeks to go until his final essay was due to be handed in. He had started it, deleted it and restarted it countless times. He was never happy with his writing, and was angry with himself for "failing" at this task, as he viewed it. He wanted his last essay to be perfect, to blow people away, be original and outstanding.

Zack knew he could do something special, but he was never satisfied with what he drafted. He kept telling himself that he was useless for not being able to craft a beautiful essay, and that he didn't deserve his degree if he couldn't do this properly. He was late handing in his essay as he procrastinated and struggled so much to complete the work.

If you recognize yourself and your behaviour in Zack's story or your perfectionist tendencies are having a negative negative impact on you, read on to find out more about techniques you can try straightaway.

## Top tips to manage perfectionism

**Ask if there are workshops or help available for perfectionism at your university**

Helping students with perfectionist tendencies is becoming an increasing challenge for university communities and more and more support is being provided. There are specific CBT-related techniques that can help to break the cycle, too, so check to see if you can find help that includes these.

### Exercise self-compassion

This does **not** mean self-pity or self-indulgence.

Self-compassion is a concept whereby you are as kind and caring to yourself as you are to a good friend (Neff, 2018).

You don't need to suffer, push on through or be stoic. You can:

- Take the time to be kind to yourself
- Recognize that you are struggling and look after your own feelings
- Keep doing the things you want to be doing to ensure that you can function and feel well
- Make an active effort to stop criticizing yourself
- Check out the website by Oscar-winning Aardman Animation – Whatsupwitheveryone.com – to watch brilliant examples of the challenges that can trip students up in everyday life, including perfectionism.

**Human beings are not perfect; it's one of our most endearing traits. So, embrace your imperfections and unique qualities.**

## The Continuum technique

This technique involves adjusting what you consider to be "good enough", moving from "perfection" to "acceptable" or "good". Currently, you only consider *perfection* to be good enough, so we need to dial that down to what is **actually** good enough.

Start by aiming to complete a draft of the task which is "good enough". If you then have some time before the deadline, work on it in small chunks, improving sections bit by bit. If time runs out, you can hand it in – even though it may not be perfect, it will be good enough and on time!

This approach reduces pressure on you, and also reduces the risk of procrastination.

You can design your own continuum (using the diagram below as an example) depending on your type of work or study, but the process will help you to agree with yourself what would be "good enough".

You can then let go of unrealistic expectations (the far-right end of the continuum line below).

"Good enough" might be getting *65%* not 85%, or writing about a topic that inspires and interests you but that you don't have time to read *everything* about (but you have read enough to be able to say something genuinely engaged and enthusiastic (and maybe even original!)). Try to think what "doing okay" would look like for you.

When you can find "good enough", you will have a lot more peace (and time!) in your life, but it can take time to adjust.

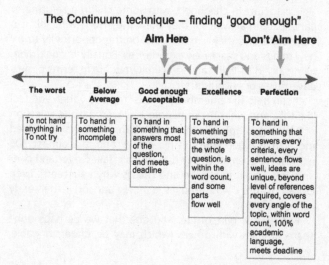

The Continuum technique – finding "good enough"

| The worst | Below Average | Good enough Acceptable | Excellence | Perfection |
|---|---|---|---|---|
| To not hand anything in To not try | To hand in something incomplete | To hand in something that answers most of the question, and meets deadline | To hand in something that answers the whole question, is within the word count, and some parts flow well | To hand in something that answers every criteria, every sentence flows well, ideas are unique, beyond level of references required, covers every angle of the topic, within word count, 100% academic language, meets deadline |

Aim Here

Don't Aim Here

**Fear of failure / making mistakes**

Closely linked to perfectionism is the fear of making mistakes or "failing".

Students are often very worried about being seen to "fail", even though what *they* view as "failure" may actually be a relatively straightforward, common or understandable mistake, *not* a disaster.

They can dread **feedback**, even though this is essential for all of us to improve in life and achieve what we want to achieve, such as a good degree, a great project, an innovative approach to an old problem in a PhD, and so on.

Young people are also often terrified of **letting other people down** – their parents, families, carers, friends, and sometimes tutors or teachers too. They worry about what others will think of them, and this in turn creates more stress and tendency toward perfectionism, or it can also create a complete block and avoidance of the piece of work or activity (such as a competitive sport).

It can start in childhood, with some children refusing to participate in activities if they think they won't win. This is a huge shame as they can miss out on the opportunity to try new things and share new experiences. Equally, in adulthood, being afraid to "fail" can really limit your life in terms of new adventures or encounters.

It can help to remember famous "failures" when you feel like this, and what those people achieved despite rejection or setback. People like Michael Jordan, who says he missed more than 9,000 shots in his career and lost almost 300 games. He goes on to say that he has "failed over and over and over again in my life and that is why I succeed". Even Oprah Winfrey was fired as a news anchor in her early career!

Failure is a part of life, and one that we perhaps don't share enough with others (which may be understandable, even though it would be helpful), but those experiences are key to how we learn, so try not to fear "failure", and instead use every mistake and every opportunity for feedback to help shape your work to make it better.

---

### Top tips if fear of failure is holding you back

- Don't avoid trying new things or things you may feel are out of your comfort zone because you might not be brilliant at them or you might "fail".
- Take "good risks". This might include choosing an unfamiliar but interesting topic to study for a short module or student-led project, applying for a role that is likely to stretch you but be enjoyable, or research something that will be challenging and may not work out but will be rewarding as a process.
- View mistakes and when things go wrong as all part of the learning experience of university or life.
- If things go wrong, take time to feel upset, but then take a breath, meet a friend to complain about it, deal with it, do some exercise, sleep on it, and try to move on, if it is not of genuine life-and-death significance.

---

### Unrealistic expectations and time-management issues (or "work is all-consuming")

Do you ever feel as though you haven't got enough time for all the things you need (let alone want!) to do? Do you hand work in late (or get close to doing so) on a regular basis? Do you live and breathe your thesis or academic work? Do you find it hard to switch off from all your activities, including your studies?

You may be suffering from unrealistic expectations of what you can manage and / or poor time management.

These are issues that can affect all sorts of students when juggling deadlines, having creative ideas, prepping for exams, keeping up with extracurricular or family activities, social engagements, and university events.

It is common for students to take on or sign up to loads of things, then spend their entire time rushing about yelling, "I'm so busy! I haven't got enough time!"

Deadlines slide, the weeks race by and, before you know it, exam time's arrived and you're in a panic because you've spent too much time on non-academic activities, or not quite got the balance right on your different academic modules and workloads.

Help is at hand!

Again, time management is an issue that is well recognized by universities, and these are certainly skills that will stand you in good stead for life. This is why most institutions run time management and academic planning skills training workshops for their students. All you have to do is enquire and sign up (and actually go)!

Some universities have run "You are not your thesis" campaigns to address the risk of over-immersing yourself in academic study, and they also tackle difficulties with supervisors, low motivation and "second-year blues", so it might be helpful to seek out advice on these topics if they are getting you down.

If you feel you can't talk to your supervisor, try putting it in writing, and if that doesn't work, seek out post- grad support groups locally or online for relevant advice. Websites like thewellbeingthesis.org.uk are useful wherever you study as a postgrad.

**Top tips for good time management**

Try these tips to get life back under control and set yourself realistic expectations:

- Take a good hard look at what you need to be doing and what you are doing because it's fun / good for your CV. Prune back a couple of activities that might be less essential to create some time. You can always do them again in the future!

- Ask for academic support from your tutor / supervisor early on, especially about planning work / prioritizing modules / deadlines and so on.

- Draw up a timetable on a spreadsheet with all your deadlines / exams etc. written in so that you have a clear timeline. Then, write in when certain tasks have to be done by in preparation for meeting the final deadlines, e.g., "Read this paper in time for writing such and such essay".

- Work with friends (if you find it helpful) to learn together, be creative together or practise together, as you'll be more likely to sit down and do the work if you have committed to do it with someone else. It can be fun too, of course.

- Schedule some treats for when you achieve something on your planner, for example, a cinema trip or pizza night with friends.

- Use time-management apps.

- Build in time to exercise, relax and eat healthy snacks, as well as see other people (in person!). It is so important to stay well when working and juggling your busy life!

## Imposter phenomenon

If you have ever felt like "everyone else is cleverer than me, a faster reader than me, better than me at this topic", or as though you "don't deserve to be at this university" and that you are a "fish out of water", then you may have imposter phenomenon.

You are not alone.

It is quite common to feel like you are the odd one out, and that someone is at any moment going to point out that you shouldn't be here, that there's been a mistake, and would you please just leave the course / university etc.

Students who have arrived with a scholarship, or through less-traditional routes, to higher education can be particularly prone to imposter phenomenon, as can those in a minority group or from overseas.

You might feel as if have no idea what you're doing, and that someone is bound to notice soon. You perhaps forget that you had to go through a selection process in order to get into university, and that you have as much right to be there as anyone else, as well as the absolute ability and potential to achieve great things.

Some of our most well-known Hollywood stars have talked about how they sometimes feel like this. Emma Stone said, "I sometimes feel like an imposter and think 'why do I deserve to be here?'" (Zarya, 2017), and Ryan Reynolds has had similar feelings, saying, "To be honest, I still feel like a freckle-faced kid, faking it until I make it" (Strategic Mentors, 2022).

**Top tips to overcome imposter phenomenon**

Imposter phenomenon is common, and once you know what it is, you can:

- **Acknowledge** your feelings and share them with others who you trust
- **Think about what you are good at** (give yourself a pat on the back for that!)
- **Remind yourself** that you were good enough to get where you are now
- **Stop comparing yourself** with others; they may have had a very different journey to yours to arrive in higher education
- **Set yourself realistic goals** that, when achieved, will reinforce what you are good at and boost your confidence (Oxford University)

**Remember, you are *not* a fraud and you *do* deserve to be here, along with all the success that will follow.**

# CHAPTER 6

# PERSONAL PROBLEMS

Some of the issues that affect students are related to their personal lives, including feeling homesick, worrying about their own identity, money stress, or more commonly than you might think, struggling with their purpose in life. The good news is that universities are full of people waiting to help you with such problems, from the Students' Union and Chaplaincy to the counseling team and doctors. Just ask them for confidential advice if you're finding it tough.

**Homesickness**

It doesn't matter where you're from or how far (or not) you are from home: students often get homesick. It's not uncommon for doctors to see homesick students whose families live less than an hour from the university and who go home at every opportunity they can. They will likely also have looked after lots of students from overseas who not only have to deal with the academic demands of university, but have to do so in a new language, culture, climate and in foreign surroundings.

### Top tips if you're feeling homesick

- **Try not to go home for at least the first four weeks of term** – it is very common to feel a bit displaced and lonely at first, but if you possibly can, try not to go home for at least the first four weeks of university term if you are living away from home and free of caring responsibilities. This will allow you to settle in better, meet other students, go to events and start feeling like you belong in this new institution. Going home after that is perfectly reasonable and you shouldn't try to "push through" and not go home at all if you want to and would feel better for doing so.
- **Get involved in workshops** – many universities run workshops for homesick students to help them settle in. Some organize multiple activities to build your social networks. So, give these a try, and even if some of them are not your natural environment or make you feel a bit uncertain, they might lead to meeting a new friend, or finding out about a new activity that would otherwise have passed you by.
- **Ask your family to send small care packages** – some students like to receive parcels including favourite snacks, magazines or a packet of good coffee. This might be a good idea for you as long as it doesn't make you feel more homesick.
- **Plan ahead** – it can be helpful to plan visits home, or welcome visitors from home every few weeks, or even planning for the holidays if it's too far to travel during term time, of course.

- **Create a home WhatsApp group** – this can be a nice way to feel part of discussions and chat about home life, without actually being there – again, as long as it doesn't make you miss them too much and isn't all-consuming.
- **Stay busy** – not locked away in your room, and make sure you meet people and explore your new surroundings to gradually reduce the feelings of missing home.
- If the homesickness doesn't seem to be wearing off gradually and you are feeling more down, flat or numb, even after several weeks have passed, then don't hesitate to **seek help and talk to a professional about it**; this feeling can progress to a more depressive type of episode for some people if ignored.

## Identity (self / new / changing)

Being a young adult arriving at a new university creates a moment of real opportunity to establish your self-identity. You can create a "new you": try out a new persona, or explore your sexuality, gender, race and culture in ways that may never have been possible previously, and in an environment that is likely to be tolerant and supportive of it.

This wonderful new freedom to be yourself or curate the "new you" can also bring conflict of course, as your family, friends from home and perhaps some of your new contacts adjust (or not) to the new reality.

**You no longer fit into the you-shaped hole you left behind.**

It may be helpful therefore to *talk* about your thoughts and ideas, and any plans you may have to change your appearance or emphasize certain aspects of it, with those people who are most likely to be affected *prior* to changes occurring (if you can).

Break it to them gently if possible.

---

### Top tips for establishing a new you

- Drop hints about your changes and try to remember that just because it feels right for you, it may not feel right yet for everyone who loves you (even if it should).
- If your appearance has changed, can you share photos before someone sees you in person, or at least let them know in advance?
- If your politics or values have shifted, try to have gentle conversations around the topic, or accept that you might have to avoid it on occasion to keep the peace, if your views are unlikely to be shared.
- If you have become vegan, don't assume that others have to cook to your tastes and choices – be prepared to help out by offering to bring your own food initially.
- It won't always be easy but try to **be considerate about how you reveal the new you**, and of the impact it might have on relationships and established views / politics / religious choices. Your choices may be seen as a criticism of another person's life choices, even if that's not how it's meant, and being aware of this can allow for a diplomatic approach where possible.

---

Many doctors will unfortunately have witnessed and supported students though dreadful breakdowns in family relations as they established their new identities or lifestyles in direct conflict with their parents' beliefs or understanding.

The students were absolutely not at fault, and prior discussion might not have changed the parents' feelings or the overall outcomes, but it is always worth trying to talk things through in life.

They will sadly also have known students to take their own lives when they felt unable to be themselves or live true to their sexuality or beliefs, and such heartbreaking events might have been avoided (we will never know) if the young person had felt accepted and supported by society, their community or their family. If you recognize this conflict in yourself, please do talk to the university's wellbeing support staff, who are absolutely committed to *helping you to be you*.

## Lack of purpose or reason for being, also known as an "existential crisis"

Interestingly, counselors and doctors will see many students over the years who are deeply troubled by their lack of purpose in life, their feeling that the world seems pointless, or their belief that life is a charade or has no meaning for them.

Clearly there can be close links with depression in some of these beliefs and feelings, but often those young people will have thought about the meaning of life for many months or years, and have not yet been able to find a meaning for themselves.

They have then become quite low and, in some rare cases, thought about ending their lives because of this lack of purpose or reason for living. For them suicide seems a rational decision, made after prolonged deliberation and consideration of their future options.

**Lack of purpose or direction can actually be one of the most serious risks to young people's mental health so you should definitely seek support if this feels like you.**

## Damon's story

Damon was a 20-year-old second-year student when he saw the counseling service. He seemed very flat and his manner was subdued. His housemates had encouraged him to speak to someone, and were in the waiting room. They had become increasingly concerned about his comments, which were along the lines of "What's the point? There's no reason for me to be here. I might as well not be." He had not been enjoying his course and couldn't see where it might take him. He had no idea what he wanted to do with his life and was beginning to think that he had no purpose or reason for carrying on.

The counselor listened, and explained that it was not uncommon for young adults to still be looking for their purpose in life and that sometimes it could take a few years to settle on a reason for being, a reason to get up every day and go to work, volunteer, or be active in the world. The counselor suggested that Damon speak to the careers service for some new ideas about work opportunities or experience, as well as taking time to think about doing something for others that might give him a renewed sense of achievement, such as volunteering at a local kids' charity, or at a homeless or animal shelter.

They agreed to keep talking and see what other ideas they could come up with that might help him to rediscover his motivation and commitment to "keep going while seeing where life took him".

Are you having an existential crisis or struggling to feel a sense of purpose?

It's not so much "I'm so hopeless, I feel so awful, things will never get better, what's the point in carrying on?" but more:

"Life is pointless, there doesn't seem to be any greater purpose or reason for me to be here, I'm not contributing anything useful, what's the point in carrying on?"

## Solutions and strategies

If you recognize the latter sentiments, then yes, you may well be struggling with your reason for living – although if you are having either of these conversations with yourself, you should certainly talk to a health and wellbeing expert such as a doctor, counselor, psychologist or other student support professional soon in order to share your emotions and find ways to feel better and work through them.

But you are not alone, and such feelings have even been given the name "quarter-life crisis" – though this seems a little dismissive of what can present as very serious psychological distress, and which professionals are always happy to talk through with any struggling student.

It can take time, but with support, counseling or therapy, young adults can come through a questioning and often confusing period and emerge the other side with a new perspective on their purpose in life (which may not yet be clearly defined, but which will evolve and take shape with the coming years).

## Set goals

This can be useful as a technique if you've lost your way. Setting goals, even just bite-sized "mini goals", can give you a sense of purpose when you are feeling lost. These might include anything from having a daily shower (if you've been feeling really low), to meeting a friend for coffee, or reading two chapters of a book.

Setting goals is recognized to improve what psychologists call "self-agency", defined as "the ability to have control over your actions", or your "free will" – essentially, control over your life's direction and choices.

If you set yourself goals, and then choose to engage and achieve them, this will positively feedback and make you feel better about yourself, as well as underline the fact that you are in charge of what you do and have that control and direction over your life. You can shift your focus from having a "life purpose" to having a daily or weekly purpose, which may feel much more achievable and rewarding. Let's look at a few goal-setting examples.

- If you set your goal as walking around the block every day, and you do this, and slowly you start to feel better (for being outside, for seeing other people in passing, for getting the exercise), then you can give yourself a pat on the back after a couple of weeks, and know that you can do this one thing. Next time you might then try to walk a little further, through a park or to some stores.
- Another goal, if you are feeling very lost and low in your emotions, might be to go online and book a counseling or doctor's appointment to talk about how you're feeling. Ask someone to help you if it feels overwhelming but you would like to go, and maybe take a friend or family member with you. The goal after that may then be to keep going back for follow-up appointments, or to start therapy.

It is important to set *realistic* goals; you don't want to set yourself up to fail, and it's good to make the goals something you can measure ("I will read two chapters", "I will book an appointment") so you know you have achieved them.

**Don't give up** if things don't go well immediately, but stick with those goals and you will feel so much better when you do achieve them.

## Financial problems

Personal finances definitely worry students at university (and their families at home), but it's not just the tuition fees that cause concerns; the cost of daily living, rent, food, clothes, and any treats such as holidays etc. create a significant amount of stress. This financial stress is recognized as being really important for students, and there are now some brilliant websites and resources to help you with what may seem like boring tasks (like budgeting), but might literally save you thousands in cash (as well as your sanity) over the next few years! The international cost-of-living crisis has had a significant impact on students (Carter, 2023), and has led some universities to provide additional support, such as food banks and hardship funds (Fox, 2023).

---

### Top tips to keep track of your finances

- **Download free budget spreadsheets** (at savethestudent.org in the UK or, in the US, College Life Made Easy) to fill in your "income" (loan, salary from part-time jobs, savings, monetary gifts at birthday and Christmas).
- **Write down everything you spend**, so that you can see if it balances out. It can be eye-opening to see how much those lattes and lunches add up to!
- **Set monthly and yearly smart goals for yourself** (find downloadable guides at Blackbullion.com).
- **Research the various types of student bank accounts available** – some of them even include deals and incentives (in the UK, try moneysavingexpert.com and in the US, check out the

Times Higher Education guide to international student bank accounts).

- **Get an overdraft** on your bank account if possible (but be careful not to abuse it, as this can make matters worse).

The websites mentioned above also have great top tips for saving on daily expenses, such as:

- **Making your own lunches** and taking them with you
- **Cycling** instead of taking public transport
- **Doing surveys and market research** for cash and tokens at the university
- **Getting cheap haircuts** by being the trainee hairdresser's guinea pig
- **Getting discount, loyalty and membership cards** wherever possible
- **Shopping the reduced sections** in stores and supermarkets

There are so many apps to help save you money – again, check out savethestudent.org and blackbullion.com and collegelifemadeeasy.com for more advice.

## What next for your financial planning?

As with many challenges, the key is to plan ahead, not bury your head in the sand and think about possible ways to save money that suit your life but feel realistic. Even students on full-time courses are getting part-time jobs to earn a little money; but this is stressful, so you could consider working in the holidays instead, if possible, to earn some cash for the year ahead, or looking for on-campus jobs to reduce time travelling to work.

Or how about babysitting for one of your lecturers, tutoring local kids, dog walking at weekends, house sitting and so on?

## Feeling financially flat?
### Don't hide away!

If you are feeling the financial stress, don't shut yourself away and stop socializing to "save money", as this will just make you feel worse. Find activities that are free or very cheap, go running instead of to a gym, and stay active and connected to others, while using the savings tips mentioned in this chapter. The Money Advice team at your university may be a good place to start if your money worries are getting too much.

---

### In summary

Some of these personal or financial problems can feel all too much, and make everyday life a struggle. By setting yourself small, achievable goals it may be possible to manage and overcome the barriers you face, while making yourself feel better. You may need professional support, especially if the problems are making you feel very flat or lost, but the help is out there – you just need to ask. These issues are common, and can be dealt with, but everyone needs a helping hand sometimes.

# CHAPTER 7

# "TRANSITION BLUES"

Going to university, travelling for the holidays or field trips, moving accommodation, studying abroad, placements, leaving university for the workplace, or moving onto further academic studies... for students, the change is constant and the transitions never-ending.

It's not surprising that some students get "transition blues", ranging from post-travelling / gap year blues to graduation blues, or even transition-related depression in the more severe cases.

That feeling of being dislocated, of not quite fitting, that everyone else knows what's going on except you, or that you have experienced something that no one else can quite understand – these are all common feelings in the different scenarios and circumstances mentioned above. Going through these experiences with another person can really bond you together, but it can also mean that you feel that only *they* can truly understand your situation. This is thankfully *not* the case.

Here are some ideas on how to cope with change at different stages of life.

## Top tips to handle change

### Share your feelings

You are not alone in feeling disconnected or different at university, although it may be for reasons that differ from someone else's feelings, so remember to talk to other students. *Share* the feelings you are having, even if they haven't shared exactly the same experience, as they are likely to understand and empathize, despite the fact that their situation involved being in industry, for example, rather than Paris for a year.

### Keep busy

While it will be natural to reflect back on a happy experience and miss the people or places that made it special, it is important to rediscover a sense of purpose and drive for where you are and what you are doing *now*.

For example, if you have graduated from university and are job hunting, but feeling down that your student days are behind you, then focus your mind on what you need to be doing to polish your CV, test your interview skills, build up work experience, or do some volunteering etc., while occasionally allowing yourself a quick look at photos of your best university days. It's important to try not to wallow in them, however, or become morose that they are over, as the past is a sad and unproductive place to live. You have a fantastic future ahead of you, using your brilliant university experience to create it!

### Create new networks

When you're at school, you might imagine that school friends will be the only friends you will ever need. Then, of course, university comes along, and you meet a whole new set of people, which, over the years, you hone down to a key tribe of "university friends".

However, the process happens again as you move on into the workplace, then again if you meet your "soul mate", if and when you have kids, when you join a sports team or have a particular hobby and so on, so that, in fact, as life goes on, you will have *several* sets of supportive, reliable friends; networks that you call on or spend time with depending on your mood or situation, but who are more or less closely present over the years.

So, take these moments of **transition** as opportunities to create new networks, meet new people, test out new friendships or hobbies or interests, not ignoring your old friends of course, but adding to your web of interconnections, without necessarily knowing if those new connections will last or lead to interesting future possibilities.

## Try something new (and possibly scary!)

Coping with change is one of life's hardest challenges, and most people don't like it or find it uncomfortable. But if you can, try to see it as an **opportunity** wherever possible rather than as a threat or worry.

Look for the positives, say yes to things that might make you a little nervous but will test you too, such as job opportunities in unknown locations, or openings in organizations you might not have previously considered, or trying a new activity or team sport. Without being foolhardy or engaging in overly risky behaviour, assess the challenge and talk it through with others, plan for it, then make the leap, and do something that **stretches** you.

Try this:

### Learned optimism

Learned optimism is the concept of taking a pessimistic view of an experience and turning it into an optimistic view. It was defined by Martin Seligman in 1990 in his book *Learned Optimism*, and is part of the Positive Psychology approach.

It is about viewing difficult situations as *unlucky setbacks*, not personal slights and *not permanent* in their effect. It's about cultivating a positive outlook, being a "glass half full" kind of person. The theory is that we can develop this, we are not just *born* a pessimist or optimist.

In some ways, learned optimism is the opposite of "learned helplessness" (see the frog metaphor below), where, as things get harder, you slowly give up.

As life gets tougher, we can sometimes feel like quitting. This is where learned optimism may be a helpful technique, allowing you to view the difficult situation through a different lens, if possible.

Cognitive behavioural approaches with a therapist use this technique for conditions such as depression.

You can learn approaches such as:

- Taking time to be **grateful** for the good things in your life
- **Actively** stopping yourself when you feel yourself starting to ruminate about the bad things
- **Using positive language** and phrases
- **Surrounding yourself** with positive people

### Watch out for learned helplessness – the frog metaphor

The often-used metaphor is of the frog and a saucepan of boiling water. They say that if you put a frog in boiling water, it will, of course, jump out immediately, but that if you put it into cold water then heat it up gradually, it won't notice and will eventually die (please don't try this at home!).

The latter behaviour is essentially an example of learned helplessness.

In other words, if we are immersed in a constantly challenging situation, we may be more likely to give up than if we arrive fresh to it, and can fight back and have the energy to get ourselves out of it. This is sometimes seen with toxic relationships, which can develop over time, and lead people to stay in a difficult situation when they have lost the energy or belief that they can and should leave. Students are as likely as anyone else to have relationships which are unpleasant, co-dependent or bad for them in another way, and in the worst cases are violent or abusive, so this learned helplessness is sometimes seen at university and must not be ignored.

**The aim of learned optimism is to improve outlook and, in the longer term, your health, as optimists have better health than pessimists, and less depression**, according to Seligman. It is a useful skill, though clearly not enough in itself to cope with very difficult or challenging relationships or other scenarios, but can be helpful for dealing with change and new challenges in life such as transition.

### In summary

Transition and change are hard for most people, but it is up to you whether you view these times as threats or opportunities. By looking at such moments positively and embracing the possibilities, you will likely pass through them more successfully as well as giving yourself a better shot at good physical and mental health.

# FINAL WORDS

Throughout the course of this book, we've discovered:

- That life, and university in particular, can be complicated and challenging;
- That life changes constantly and transition is tricky;
- That it takes time to find our purpose in life;
- That pressures will come from academic work, relationships, financial hardship and our (sometimes unrealistic) expectations of ourselves, and the notions that others have of who we are and what we should be;
- That there are plenty of ways to make new friends and meet people;
- That we can be pretty tough on ourselves; that we think we are not good enough or undeserving of success, which isn't always helpful;
- But that there are many ways to manage these difficulties, if we can simply take a moment to think about what is happening around us and what we can do to tackle the situation.

You will hopefully have identified some of the specific problems you are facing and read the suggested tips, solutions or strategies to address them, or at least know when and where to get help if you need support to do this.

You may be feeling inspired to develop your growth mindset (stretch yourself), set some goals, have conversations with yourself or try some learned optimism, all of which are really useful lifelong skills to have in your **toolkit of resourcefulness**.

One final reassuring truth to think about, when despair hits, or you feel frustrated by conflict or unsure how to move forward is:

**"This too shall pass."**

It's a saying that's been around for centuries, and was used by Abraham Lincoln among others, allegedly, to acknowledge that everything is temporary.

Sometimes we all need help to remember that bad times will pass, and that, although tragic things happen, we can cope even when we feel like we can't. Everything is a phase.

Life will bring good phases and bad phases, and *both* will end, so when life is tough it can be helpful to remind ourselves that the tough times are temporary.

Or as Winston Churchill once said, "If you're going through hell, keep going".

What does that mean for you?

Sometimes, when you're "going through hell", it can feel never-ending, relentlessly depressing and like every day is a chore.

Believe it or not, most people have known that feeling at some point in their lives, and with age and experience you usually learn that such dreadful times pass to some extent (albeit perhaps not completely), that the pain lessens and life moves forward – despite how hard this might seem when you've got your whole life ahead of you.

### How do I keep going?

Humans are extraordinarily resilient to trauma and distress, so it may help to try to remember, when things feel unendingly awful, that they *will* get better, and you may just need to get through a day (or even an hour) at a time, as well as **talk** about how you are feeling, get **professional** support, take **comfort** from other humans (or pets), and try to hold onto a shred of **hope** as you push through the days. The pandemic gave us multiple examples of getting through bleak times with the support of others (and a lot of lockdown puppies). So, if times are tough, you already know you can cope with exceptional challenges. Don't give up; reach out.

Hopefully this book has offered the reassurance that you are not alone, the knowledge that there are things that you can do and that your future is very much in your control; and that it will have inspired you to get there more happily and feeling healthier.

If you need extra support, that is completely normal and understandable; we are all human, we all go through difficult times, and we all need a helping hand sometimes.

University is a place to learn – not just academically, but also about life and how to manage when the going gets tough.

Universities are filled with helpful souls whose jobs involve supporting students, so reach out and ask if you need help, or get a friend or family member to help you onto that first step of the path, if you feel unable to do it alone.

Either is fine, but **do** reach out, please don't suffer in silence.

You *can* do this. It *can* get better.

# ADDITIONAL RESOURCES

**TED talks**

- Carol Dweck – "The Power of Believing That You Can Improve"
- Russell Foster – "Why Do We Sleep?"
- Sarah Jayne Blakemore – "The Mysterious Workings of the Adolescent Brain"
- Dominique Thompson – "What I Learnt from 78,000 GP Consultations with University Students"
- Thomas Curran – "Our Dangerous Obsession with Perfectionism Is Getting Worse"

**FODMAP diet for irritable bowel syndrome**

https://www.theibsnetwork.org/diet/fodmaps/

**Money advice**

www.blackbullion.com
www.savethestudent.org
https://collegelifemadeeasy.com

**Perfectionism**

https://www.cci.health.wa.gov.au/Resources/Looking-After-Yourself/Perfectionism
www.whatsupwitheveryone.com
https://ray.yorksj.ac.uk/id/eprint/2966/1/Perfectionism%20fact%20sheet.pdf

## Apps

- *Student Health App* – for all health matters
- *CBT-I apps* – for insomnia
- *distrACT* – for self-harm
- *Headspace* – for mindfulness
- *SAM* – for anxiety

## Websites

- NHS support **www.nhs.uk**
- **Mental Health America** mhanational.org/get-involved/ contact-us
- jedfoundation.org **in the US**
- **Suicidal crisis or self-harm in the USA** 988lifeline.org
- Mind **www.mind.org.uk** or call **0300 123 3393**
- Money Saving Expert **www.moneysavingexpert.com**
- Moodgym (for CBT skills) **www.moodgym.com.au**
- Student Minds (the UK national student mental health charity) **www.studentminds.org.uk**
  ADHD **www.adhdfoundation.org.uk**
- Autism **www.autism.org.uk**
- Gender issues **www.mermaidsuk.org.uk**
- LGBT+ **www.stonewall.org.uk**

## Social media

Dr Julie Smith **www.tiktok.com/@drjuliesmith**

# REFERENCES

**Bembenutty, H.** (2011). Academic delay of gratification and academic achievement. Available at: https://ssrlsite.files.wordpress.com/2018/01/bembenutty-2011-academic-delay-of-grat-and-academic-achievement.pdf

**Bhardwa, S.** (2023). A guide to international student bank accounts in the US. Available at: https://www.timeshighereducation.com/student/advice/guide-international-student-bank-accounts-us

**Blackwell, L., Trzesniewski, K. & Dweck, C.** (2007). Implicit Theories of Intelligence Predict Achievement Across an Adolescent Transition: A Longitudinal Study and an Intervention. *Child Development*. 78(1), 246–63. Available at: https://www.mtoliveboe.org/cmsAdmin/uploads/blackwell-theories-of-intelligence-child-dev-2007.pdf

**Bouchrika, I.** (2023). 75 College Drug Abuse Statistics: 2021/2023 Data, Facts & Predictions. Available at: https://research.com/education/college-drug-abuse-statistics

**Carey, B.** (2015). *How We Learn*. New York, NY: Random House.

**Carter, G.** (2023). Student voices: the cost of living crisis. Available at: https://www.suttontrust.com/news-opinion/all-news-opinion/student-voice-cost-of-living/

**Curran, T. & Hill, A.** (2017). Perfectionism is increasing over time: A meta-analysis of birth cohort differences from 1989 to 2016. *Psychological Bulletin*.

**Cushnahan, M.** (2022). Navigating University As A Non-Drinking Student. Available at: https://www.studentbeans.com/blog/uk/navigating-university-as-a-sober-student/

**Duckworth, A.** (2016). *Grit*. London: Vermillion.

**Dweck, C. & Leggett, E.** (1988). A social cognitive approach to motivation and personality. *Psychological Review*. 95(2), 256–73.

**Fox, G.** (2023). More than a quarter of universities have student food banks, reveals research. Available at: https://www.independent.co.uk/news/uk/home-news/universities-student-food-banks-cost-of-living-crisis-b2411249.html

**Higher Education Policy Institute.** (2018). Most students think taking illegal drugs causes problems for users as well as society and want their universities to take a tougher stance. Available at: https://www.hepi.ac.uk/2018/06/12/students-think-taking-illegal-drugs-causes-problems-users-well-society-want-universities-take-tougher-stance/

**Hystad, S., Eid, J., Laberg, J., Johnsen, B. & Bartone, P.** (2009). Academic Stress and Health: Exploring the Moderating Role of Personality Hardiness. *Scandinavian Journal of Educational Research*. 53(5), 421–29.

**Jose, P., Ryan, N. & Pryor, J.** (2012). Does Social Connectedness Promote a Greater Sense of Well-Being in Adolescence Over Time? *Journal of Research on Adolescence*. 22(2), 235–51.

**MedlinePlus.** Tips for Getting a Good Night's Sleep. Available at: https://medlineplus.gov/magazine/issues/summer15/articles/summer15pg22.html

**Mind.** (2019). Five ways to wellbeing. Available at: https://www.mind.org.uk/workplace/mental-health-at-work/taking-care-of-yourself/five-ways-to-wellbeing/

**National Confidential Inquiry into Suicide and Safety in Mental Health.** (2017). Suicide by children and young people. Available at: https://sites.manchester.ac.uk/ncish/reports/suicide-by-children-and-young-people/

**National Confidential Inquiry into Suicide and Safety in Mental Health.** (2018). Annual report 2018: England, Northern Ireland, Scotland and Wales. Available at: https://sites.manchester.ac.uk/ncish/reports/annual-report-2018-england-northern-ireland-scotland-and-wales/

**Neff, K.** (2018). Self-Compassion. Available at: https://self-compassion.org

**O'Connell, M.** (2017). Why We Sleep by Matthew Walker review – how more sleep can save your life. Available at: https://www.theguardian.com/books/2017/sep/21/why-we-sleep-by-matthew-walker-review

**Open University.** (2018). Active reading. Available at: http://www2.open.ac.uk/students/skillsforstudy/active-reading.php

**Oppong, T.** (2018). The Theory of "Grit" as a Predictor of Success in Life. Available at: https://medium.com/personal-growth/the-theory-of-grit-as-a-    predictor-of-success-in-life-24274ceec46

**Rasch, D.** (2018). The Procrastination Wheel of Suffering: Part Five – Anxiety, Deadlines and Binge Writing. Available at:    https://davidraschphd.wordpress.com/2018/05/02/the-procrastination-wheel-of-suffering-part-five-anxiety-deadlines-and-binge-writing/

**SC, K.** (1979). Stressful life events, personality, and health: an inquiry into hardiness. Available at: https://www.ncbi.nlm.nih.gov/pubmed/458548

**Seligman, M.** (1990). *Learned Optimism.* New York, NY: Knopf.

**Strategic Mentors.** (2022). Think you're not good enough? Here's proof that you are. Available at: https://strategicmentors.co.uk/think-youre-not-good-enough/

**Thompson, D.** (2018). What I Learnt from 78,000 GP Consultations with University Students. Available at: https://www.youtube.com/watch?v=gt-ToFPHCkI

**University of Oxford.** Expectations, Transitions and Overcoming Imposter Syndrome. Available at: https://www.ox.ac.uk/sites/files/oxford/field/field_document/

**Van Edwards, V.** (2018). Learn How to Make Friends As An Adult Using These 5 Steps. Available at: https://www.scienceofpeople.com/how-to-make-friends/

**Walker, M.** (2017). *Why We Sleep*. London: Allen Lane.

**Zarya, V.** (2017). Why Emma Stone is a Poster Child for 'Impostor Syndrome'. Available at: https://fortune.com/2017/09/20/emma-stone-battle-sexes-imposter/

# TriggerHub is one of the most elite and scientifically proven forms of mental health intervention

Trigger Publishing is the leading independent mental health and wellbeing publisher in the UK and US. Our collection of bibliotherapeutic books and the power of lived experience changes lives forever. Our courageous authors' lived experiences and the power of their stories are scientifically endorsed by independent federal, state and privately funded research in the US. These stories are intrinsic elements in reducing stigma, making those with poor mental health feel less alone, giving them the privacy they need to heal, ensuring they are guided by the essential steps to kick-start their own journeys to recovery, and providing hope and inspiration when they need it most.

Clinical and scientific research conducted by assistant professor Dr Kristin Kosyluk and her highly acclaimed team in the Department of Mental Health Law & Policy at the University of South Florida (USF), as well as complementary research by her peers across the US, has independently verified the power of lived experience as a core component in achieving mental health prosperity. Their findings categorically confirm lived experience as a leading method in treating those struggling with poor mental health by significantly reducing stigma and the time it takes for them to seek help, self-help or signposting if they are struggling.

Delivered through TriggerHub, our unique online portal and smartphone app, we make our library of bibliotherapeutic titles and other vital resources accessible to individuals and organizations anywhere, at any time and with complete privacy, a crucial element of recovery. As such, TriggerHub is the primary recommendation across the UK and US for the delivery of lived experiences.

At Trigger Publishing and TriggerHub, we proudly lead the way in making the unseen become seen. We are dedicated to humanizing mental health, breaking stigma and challenging outdated societal values to create real action and impact. Find out more about our world-leading work with lived experience and bibliotherapy via triggerhub.com, or by joining us on:

🐦 @triggerhub_

📘 @triggerhub.org

📷 @triggerhub_

Dr Kristin Kosyluk, PhD, is an assistant professor in the Department of Mental Health Law and Policy at USF, a faculty affiliate of the Louis de la Parte Florida Mental Health Institute, and director of the STigma Action Research (STAR) Lab. Find out more about Dr Kristin Kosyluk, her team and their work by visiting:

USF Department of Mental Health Law & Policy:
www.usf.edu/cbcs/mhlp/index.aspx

USF College of Behavioral and Community Sciences:
www.usf.edu/cbcs/index.aspx

STAR Lab: www.usf.edu/cbcs/mhlp/centers/star-lab/

For more information, visit **BJ-Super7.com**

Printed in the USA
CPSIA information can be obtained
at www.ICGtesting.com
JSHW032055090724
66138JS00007B/41